Dear Nancy & Ben,
My these poems take you on

Overhead from Longing

a "wild and mysterious flight"

Happy Reading!

Love,

Judy

Overhead from Longing

Poems by Judith Alexander Brice

David Robert Books

Published by David Robert Books
P.O. Box 541106
Cincinnati, OH 45254-1106

ISBN: 978-1-62549-285-2

Poetry Editor: Kevin Walzer
Business Editor: Lori Jareo

Visit us on the web at www.davidrobertbooks.com

I would like to dedicate this book to four people who have been outstanding inspirations to me throughout the years—including three masterful poets, Maria Mazziotti Gillan, who started me on this amazing journey of writing poetry, Sheila Kelly who has, with her great tutelage, helped inspire many of the enclosed poems, and most of all, my wonderful poet/husband, Charles W. Brice, who has been with me every step of the way. Lastly, this book is dedicated to my artist/son, Ariel Brice, who has taught me the meaning of listening to art.

To all of you, I will remain forever grateful.

Sometimes, I am startled out of myself
like this morning, when the wild geese came squawking,
flapping their rusty hinges, and something about their trek
across the sky made me think about my life, the places
of brokenness, the places of sorrow, the places where grief has strung me
out to dry…
[and yet]
They stitch up the sky, and it is whole again.

—Barbara Crooker, *Radiance*
(italicized line, mine)

Table of Contents

Berries, Bittersweet

Snaps of Time

With Grace, The Seasons

Echoes —

Notes

Acknowledgements

Berries, Bittersweet

The geese stitch up the sky[1]

Or is it each and every one of the birds—
not just the flying geese—
but our warbler, oriole and kite
who in our dimmest, darkest hours,
can frisk our pockets of despair?

All of a sudden, when our shifting glance
has turned and they wing off to soar,
do they twist the brilliant weave of sun—
his light and beguiling thread—
into a diamond dazzle of hallowed beads–
with full sparkling, crystal core?

And before we even see, do these agile, radiant friends
steal our stash of pent-up woes,
our places of distress,
then slyly slip gnarled nuggets of gold—
of hope—
in hand and out of sight?

Most of all I wonder
will we afford this startle
out of our indifferent selves
to take this slake of longing,
to honor these flying messengers from space,
these shimmering glints of grace?

Berries, Bittersweet

Before you know what kindness
really is you must lose things...
—*from "Kindness" by Naomi Shihab Nye*

After they'd split my brain,
mended the artery that burst
asunder and left me without
whispers and thoughts,
it was only your kindness, my therapist,
that cajoled me back,
together with Kiri's lilt, Galway's flute
and *Danny Boy*—
yes, coaxed me
to listen to song and words
so I might speak again
consonant by consonant,
syllable by syllable,
word by word.

And when you, my husband,
have witnessed me go suddenly blind,
need the curtains down, the lights
turned off, what tenderness takes you,
touches you again and beyond
to fetch the ice
for my migrainous head,
the towel for my sick torment?
Such, your kindness.

As, that time you, my delicate
companion, my tiny feline gray one,
gave up your last and silent
breath and left us.
Then, as if by chance, that very day
your feathered partner came,
displayed his full bluebird glory
for us to see and tapped in code
at the freezing, attic window,
even pecked at the bittersweet
berries, blown on the sill.

The Circle Closes

You, too, would say: yes, she's a star, Earth,[2]
and when you spoke to me from love in her dialect
of dream, from out of my sleep, I did not believe
but wondered how can I answer, and how do I tell you
of the sailing boats going by on the river, the cobalt
current already far from the lake under tamaracks,
their arched arms barely covering the sun.

How do I tell you, I wondered, that your name
is inscribed in my heart, my thoughts and what I see.
How do I tell you of the beauty of this river,
her bunting blues, these languages, the water's flow,
her tongues of sand and salt, as they relay the space
of wind. So when I wake, I hold to myself wishes
for a meeting place— on land, by air, on line—.

Then, dawn morning comes, new ideas harken
back to old encounters, years before when you
went one way, and I, the other— I linger
on every desire, every birdsong,
harbor new resolve to find you,
tell you about the green hemlocks
in the dream, the pines reaching up to grasp them.

But distraction intrudes: bills, phone calls, email.
That very day, the message comes—
the circle closes when I discover
that cancer grabbed
your shortened life and won.

Lake Michigan—
Silent, Silent Now

As when a sand-piper skips
alone along a sandy shore,
next to the empty roar of waves
viewed from inside a closed window—

Silent as a lone lighthouse
outside on the jetty
beside the blowing birch,
the whiffled, whiskered grass—

Silent as this poem
while you are reading,
quiet as your thoughts
while you are thinking—

as when these words
float you to the clouds,
where they meet the lake,
the hovering gulls and sun.

Around a Bend

Like a baby
camel
with knobby knees
start,
start your wobbly life
slow,
no gratuity for you—
no marzipan flowers
on your doorstep—

a tiny tummy,
not even a hefty hump
on your back
to nourish you
or take up
the slack
of your growing life.

Seconds, minutes, hours
(you'll hear "days")
won't always be
on your side—
in fact you may forget
them, lose them,
wish them gone.

But as time slides by,
if you can wait,

you might come upon
a wintry lake encrusted
with the softest,
deepest snow and soon,
though quickly
around a bend, you'll discover
a herd of deer

standing stark,
standing still
beside a sleigh
as they watch, wait for you.

To Charlie, Beyond the Mist

*Will the mist have vanished from the lake
by the time you read this?* — *birthday note
to Charlie, June 7, 2012, from a good friend*

What she couldn't know was your eyes
warm with the June wind, as you watch
the pond's riffles, listen to them beyond
the call of terns, as they await a sign,
a shimmer, to plummet for perch straight

down through the evening sky. No, she couldn't
know your unwavering eyes focused
on your book, as your fingers leaf the pages

slowly, steady through your gaze, looking
at the script, then up once more marking
the mist, the pines, the turning call.

Too, she couldn't feel your evening
touch, tender and close, as you and I sit
entranced by the woodpecker, the primeval
scarlet-crested, pileated one, focused on his suet
oblivious to us, breeze quivering the leaves.

Mourning Calls

From beyond the brume,
beyond the horizon, she swims,
the mallard's mate,
a wail
for a call, brief before the wait
for her next plaint, shortened and hoarse

From around the cove she floats
into the evening lake, as its restive waves
batter the reeds, tawny and coarse
among the gray, the wind-tossed rocks.
She keens, still mourning—
pleads

Out into the wind she drifts,
her westward whines without hope,
amidst the singe of twilight,
a solitary
slipping of sun, singing
its own vast and disappearing song

Before the Terns

It's always the waves I hear,
the lapping of the lake
at Walloon— perhaps the first sound
my young memory held,
before the kingfishers',
the terns' bolting splash to grab
the minnows in their purling midst.

But the waves rippling,
their swish and tickles at our feet
when we were three, four
and *grown-up* five,
these waves evolved, devolved—
even now, revolve in my thoughts
to the roaring ghosts of white-cap
blues, as after a ghastly storm
they'll choose to slam
tossed and shorn cedar trunks,
or twisted, despairing, pine limbs
onto lonely, whiplashed grass.

It is always the waves I hear—
my childhood, before the turns.

Crooked Trees

To be sure, I was happy—
though fear stalked me down
the country lane, along
the rocky roads, even
in the shade of sycamores,
their shedding bark, their
crackly leaves,
the burnt out huts—
Always the one shadowed
the other, reasons obscure,
interminable. There
was peace, tranquil— calm.

Yet around the bend,
oak trees
were long since cut
crooked, slant—
by Indians to mark a trail
and keep the white man
from discerning his way,
from decimating a stand
of forest he claimed as his,
trees he knew
belonged to each man
of his own people.

Woodpeckers, Great Horned Owls
flew through the crooked trees,
their quiet— the scaling bark,
the burnt-out huts. Larks knew

to break the silence—
Was it from boredom, hunger
or like me, did they speak
from fear—
or discontent of calm,
pulse of heart?

Migraine

When the nausea descends
I forget the sunset,
her light listing its way
west, the skeins of fuchsia
falling slowly to her knees—

And then, like a lightning bolt—
first out of fear and abrupt-fused with dread—
stabs of pain, pangs of panic, intrude,
even collude to knife my head.

Before I know, I'm trapped.

Heaving shadows blacken my mind,
mist all grass underfoot, and drench
me in fields with desolate dark—

though quickly a Towhee trill
might quaver me awake,
rustle my blighted brain,
even grab its bilious gaze

to catch silken embers of sun
as they topaz the sky.

Twelve

It happens with the whims
of chance, when *Sturm* inverts
our core: turmoil may begin
as mist but, in days, swirls,
and quick a rapid switch
of fate will hasten— as if
to tornado or hurricane.

Or faster yet the Pain
may come— a knife
incise all joy; then
wish for simple death
descends in search
of fast escape.

The doctors speak
of scales from one to ten,
with ten the very worst—
they never fathom twelve,
nor know the anguished
tumult of rampant Pain—
the terror and scorch,
the festinating dread.

Tightwire

Do or do not; there is no try.
— *Yoda*

The wire stretches out:
just shadows below— as I
grapple with pain,
death's siren voice,
yet lose myself
in vital minutes, plangent-rich.

How
to balance the onslaught
of inner attack, catastrophe
of wavering body,
threat of sudden death—
with seconds of sonorous sound.

Tightropes require precision,
decision.
Who can decide
to walk the course?

How
in the festering face
of a damning demon,
on a high-strung wire?

Quiet

Give me quiet
anguish, grief to regret
my sorrow, the brown
of my past, my sparrows,
their white tattered snow.
As I take my leave, easy
with your pity and scorn—
sore now over your silent
prophet, your bleak of speech
and effort to foretell—
I must keep my words to myself,
watch this wide and windswept beach,
and wait for tomorrow's shivering wind.

Call Me Simple— a poem in honor of Serge Kovaleski[3]

> *You may shoot me with your words…*
> *But still, like air, I'll rise.*
> *—from "Still I Rise" by Maya Angelou*

Call me simple, crippled, a gimp—
With a hitched limp, weak in my walk, I'll arise
to take you down, slap your hate— trap
your deceiving sleight of rage.

"Mr. President," you won't get ahead—
there'll be no clamor nor claque of men
to praise your spiteful gestures, your sordid words.
Few fans with ire to slake your thirst.

They'll soon fade and vanish
into their cold and scabrous souls,
their own grimed and empty minds.
I won't surmise your abhorring shadows of dark,

your source of ire, deceit or lies—
you'll not rise—
you will soon be gone: no statues to say
you're great, no speakers to praise your thoughts.

Call us simple, handicapped or gimps—
our words will long surpass the time when yours
like an ignoble, withered vine, will sink below
the ground and soon molder, suddenly lost to slime.

No Moon Shadows

I can't find your God
in the graves of my pain,
no moon shadows to pluck
from evensong
nor steel stillness
in silhouettes
of these sneaky weeks to come.
I can only feel
one long jolting scream,
too many creaking fissures
in bones once rent
and no peace
or silence in my home.

The Lowest Ebb

The lowest ebb is the turn of the tide.
—from "Loss and Gain"
by Henry Wadsworth Longfellow

Is it the lowest ebb to say goodbye
to recall the good, exhale that sigh
over our lost, our gone,
though never days forgotten—
over those times that haunt
and sneak so close around,
taunt our blistered memory's tome—
full long beyond the desperate try
to expunge a taint of laugh,
of fun, even hint of true?

The future is changed,
that for sure, when you lose
a companion, a daughter—
whether in law— or in truth.
That future is different, won't ever renew
join arms again, and smile once more.
The days to come won't be the same—
as those times when her tiny hand
slipped smooth in mine to help me up
that we might rise together again.

When she chose to leave,
she exploded our sun—
no warning, no scream, just one
long disappearing void—

leaving a vast ocean of hail,
of clouds, a mote of grief.
So now we ask ourselves if
this siren slide, this slipping ebb,
is, in fact, the end of a wail,
a turn of the tide.

Shimmying

Night and rime of frost press
hard against her window panes—
new dreams dizzy from the seep
of age, the struggle to sneak back
to life, to escape the torture,

the torment of pain
wracking, fomenting her restless
body. And through it all those dreams
jolting her awake, shimmying her
mind to new places she has

never been, not ever imagined
'til now. Yet from her sleep
she screams, and then learns
only later of her words
when her husband tells...

while her memory and focus
stray away from her now lost
and frozen mind. Still,
dreams, thoughts intrude as she
fights to see the snow drift

down and settle gently,
soft beside the yellow-billed
junco, puffed gray,
solitary, silent
upon the terrace far below.

I Want To Go Back

I want to go back to my youth again
where all is in my realm, even good health,
a new young boy and soccer games to watch—
where I can see fresh buds on trees, their flowers just behind
and in the future, many months to come
to fly headlong into years—

I want to go back to youth again, and savor my career,
to forget these days of longing, these memories
of tears. But suddenly, something happens
to my darting dance of dreams— My days revolve,
and all too quick, they turn obliquely to night.

The glass grows dim— my face becomes faint gray
and much too soon my drive to fight gets undermined
by fears. I want to go back
to my youth again, my years of hope and spring,
where each step salutes both time and zeal
and headstrong, ushers in the green.

Overhead from Longing

To Charlie, April 19, 2017

Sometimes, your voice catches me
from beyond and overhead, from your longing
love—I think of your timbre,
the tremolo and cords it strikes, reminiscent
always of starlings, their cantabile speech,
as they learned to sing— no, talk, to Mozart.

Was it he who heard
and copied their joyful trance or they
who conveyed back his sweet noise
to wrap him in a swoon of song
so sonorous that he composed concertos,
so plangent that when he wrote his resplendent

masses, he was able to catch an audience
in rapt and full attention, swoop
his listeners into an evanescent murmuration[4]
as dense and wide as the starlings,
when swiftly they disappear
into their wild and mysterious flight?

Mnemosyne's Collision

In the dream I sit
at a small desk, the red chalk
blackboard all square around
each of the room's four sides—
and my Master writes
all facts, all truths,
each detail of my long-elided life.

I try to write, to catch each verity,
each frail facet of my days elapsed
—how I started, what steps,
whom I knew, even where I went—.
After mere lengthy seconds have passed
I begin to copy down my late-found
memories, the newest bulletins,

when he in turn reaches to the next
blank side, until not just one
but all four walls are covered.
But just then, as my eyes start
to catch my life, to grasp her reality
and write it all, he once more
resumes again at the first board,

begins to erase it— everything—
each piece of news— then write down
a different splinter, a wayward scrap
of an eluding past, even

my memory of Mnemosyne's directions—
erases it all, before I can learn some
of what I have long forgotten.

His *Butterfly Effect*[5]

Try to keep your heart,[6]
save it, keep it open

as the door you lost last year
when the falling oak clobbered
your home, drove limbs
through her windows.
Save in your mind their former
view, your garden— the cobalt

Hydrangeas, the Asiatic
Lilies, bending over their own
giant Ferns, as they leaned
to protect the lavender Hostas,
tightly holding silent hands
with their best and variegated friends.

Try to keep your heart,
save it, hold it close,

when the brusque and ill-
tempered Bombast walks
through your country and acts
as if he owns it all, acts as if he
is free to turn the states he governs
into the mud flats of your yard—
into possessions he owns— free
to pulverize the flowers' lives,

eradicate the butterflies,
the Monarchs.

Try to keep your heart.

I Look at You

And your eyes speak of the sky, her brilliant
emerald blue, as she travels beyond and through
her orbit of time, as she descends to catch
us all and take us to her eternal radiance of light.
Your eyes speak of the sun, her warm
and nourishing story of hope, her dreams

of fire, of time and singing sight. Though, too,
do you not wonder at our leaders' minds
now blind to the incessant heat, the burn
of days, of grass and land that lean too heavy
on the earth, too desolate on the plains
and desperate on the deserts of sand?

I look at you and see only your eyes,
and ask myself what you understand—
and what you know? Do you, like me, feel
the taste of dust, see the squander
of sun upon retreating lakes—
the glacier snow now gone?

Twigs

Outside, the yard is a wasteland,
brown– the grass not grown
where three trees fell, and I
try now to imagine how
to plant a garden, trees again
when there are but coarse
scruffs of bush and brush,
aching for spring.

Two trees, maybe three
might do, a royal empress, a birch
perhaps— even a tulip tree
around some pampas grass,
but will they bloom before the years
sweep our lives and take us
from this forever home we knew,
we thought, to be secure?

I hear today of a friend, now failing—
snatched from her place by hypocrisies
of health— desperate, does she cling
to her glimpses, her memories of house
and self, as she holds fast
to twigs of thoughts, looks askance
through broken windows of youth,
shards of home.

Old-Switch-Panic

I try to think of how to cover the stump
of our old oak, how to pretend she hadn't fallen,
or didn't exist— I try to imagine she didn't cast
her shade to soothe my heated skin, my roiling rage,

at sickened pain who visits, minute by second,
by minute again. But the sear of sun sheds
little cover for my hate, my chewing mood
that eschews all sate. I think of surrounding

the rotten stump with Old Switch Panic Grass,
but then again will this mere camouflage
assuage my real panic, embedded deep within—
the dread that my other trees, yours as well,

won't stand tall, but just randomly fall
with or without tumult, hail or thrashing storm?
Chinese Silver Grass, Purple Fountain Grass
may also cover— but not erase the rocks

of force which too often pummel
our pressured lives, unbeknownst to us.

Death's Bridge

I have been thinking of shadows

the ones that obscured the sun,
smoky grim ones
that broke our family,
perhaps yours, too—

thinking

how mordant skies eclipsed
the Jews, Gypsies, the foreign,
the weak.

Ash clouds,
the gunmetal ones,
pewter shadows
that tore open— rent
centuries of families—
women, children, and men—
generations of them,
—cultures ruptured—

Auschwitz, Treblinka,

Ravensbrück[7]—

a German lake town
with lovely forests
where ladies were brought—
elegant young women,

pregnant women, old women,
mothers, daughters,
nursing babies, Polish women,
Jewish women, Russian women,
Gypsy women, women from Auschwitz

all

taken across a bridge
a black/RavenBridge—
given a new home

to become
German carrion—

Smoky clouds,

Ash

Escape

I didn't know I'd been missing
the reeds, their ochre/gray
reflecting off the shore, the red
winged blackbirds as they hum-screeched
softly, as if lifting tiny violins in unison
beside the windy pond— geranium blue.

I didn't know, until I ran, then swam
the river's miles to the open lake,
along the birch path, along the wafting
web of willows, blown west at first,
then east, to catch the splash of silver
clouds and gilded sun above the sky.

Only then did I realize that wild
escape was the single way to seize
sight of eagles' wings, to eye a tern's
dive into depths of waves and then its ascent
again as it returns once more to a freedom
I'd known before but long forgot.

Snaps of Time

Snaps of Time

I thought I was standing
still between the hills
and swale, the green and grass
until you told me that the sky
and clouds were moving,
catching the blue, the maps
of age, the snaps of time
and truth.

I thought I was seeing
the boulders, the rocks,
the pebbles— able to wend
my way beyond and through
the paths of years, the seconds
of hours, of weeks and youth.
But in between, the water
falls of rivers, of days, in a sudden
froze— ceased their flow,

until the cold caught me
far below, looking up,
looking down,
with no clear trail
to surmount the hill
beside the spring,
beside the beckoning
apple trees, their ice
trembling branches awaiting
a thaw of spray from frigid
thundering falls.

Unequalled — Never-Ending

In memory of Mary Ibele, 1930-2017

It could as well have been any
other day, when the old lady fixed her
eggs and sat in her rocker — beige and blue
afghan laid out on her legs
as she put out the plate of toast,
eggs and bacon on her lap.

It could as well have been the days
she went to the doctor to find out why
her belly had swelled
to twice its size
or the time she went to chemo, though
it was, in fact, later — a week beyond —

when she knew her nephew would arrive
that she got up late, and sat for breakfast,
only after dressing, after letting
her loyal golden, her Fuji[8], out for his run
in their country yard. With hair styled the day
before, she'd slipped on her favorite housecoat

and waited while she ate. After a sip of tea
she cut into one of her eggs, sunny side up.
But her seconds and hours quickly switched
to a different minute, a different space —
one where "any other day" never came —
and this moment grasped her soul's final leap,

though Fuji, her unequalled one,
wouldn't know, so he stayed by her side—
alert and patient— sat
calm and still— in never-ending fidelity
second by second, minute after minute,
fourth hour after third

while she remained in her rocker,
head bent over, cocked askew,
the plate of eggs and toast cooling fast,
at rest on her lap, until her nephew came
long into hour five, to discover
her cold body, without life or time.

Reflections on a 45th Parallel

From out of our cedar swamp she strolled,
legs a paragon of grace, sharp beak straight,
her eyes beading on prey at the river's edge.

From beside the umber cat tails, each leg
stealthy, sure of foot, she strode, steady —
each feather poised in wait for the gift of light,

of wind, the surety of time to raise her wings aloft
and take her off into uncertainty of space,
of future place in her seconds of each day.

Stolid, she strode — slow, just as a chirr
of goldfinch souls sang in praise of other
beings of grace to match this Great Blue

who soon as not they knew would emerge
in kind from the moist and boggy marsh —
our swamp so filled with emerald fronds of fern

and cedar cones it could hardly be that same
one which should be "drained" — that mire
forever filling up with dank crud, rancid sludge.

Thibaudet's Tide of Song

Trees had merged to twilight
  when our car slipped smooth
over strips of road
  —pressed on fields between
forests—and captured

the almost-night dusk
  sky from Magritte.
Slow glacial hills
  came and went
through our wilting eyes,

our sight growing
  slowly more faint
as we discovered
  ourselves focused only
on the pianist, Thibaudet.

In seconds, we were bewitched
  by Khachaturian as we vibrated
and swayed under
  the car's baton
to the lilt of his Piano Concerto.

Phrases rolled with the road—
  the *Allegro* propelled us,
the saw's vibrato in the *Andante*
  stole tears and soul
from our dim-lit eyes.

Then, as a warbler offering
  no warning, the *Allegro Brillante*
opened her throat to sing:
  notes parachuted— fell— tumbled—
on more notes, cascaded

into the dusk as they lifted
  us up over the hills
through the descending dark.
  In a single scintilla of song,
the crescendo parted the night—

permitting one radiant
  moonbeam
to claim us
  before we returned
triumphantly home.

Traveling Time with Teenie Harris in Black and White[9]

There was little gleam on city streets
near the Hill District's Centre Ave.—
mostly shades of dirt debris:
decrepit hues of moldering gray
dust-darkened ash and steel mill soot,
where cars crashed, life had crumbled,
as buildings merged, later tumbled
leaving random bricks and rocks,
grimy glass piercing deep underfoot.

Amidst these streets where stones
were strewn, Teenie saw it, saved it:
little boys with beaming marbles,
wobbly wagons, weapon-sticks—
he bore witness, snapped it all.

***

Yet he showed, as well, a different life
behind those walls near Centre Ave.—
how the doors to Crawford's smoky Grill
opened to lipstick laughter, thrills,
satin smiles, bear hugs and yes,
the chills that came when sleek
soldiers' arms draped loose around
their honeys' willow necks.

The Jazz Messengers trumpeted
Just Play in their "Work Song"
while his photos kept the beat, kept us dizzy
as we gaped at Dizzy, tantalized by cauliflower
cheeks, his scat and bebop cheeks,
as they blew brass airs of heat. Our eyes
only saw how his horn shone gold
though Teenie shot in simple film
just sharpened black and white.

And then there was Sarah,
her svelte *Body and Soul*
that Teenie caressed, praised, even
lauded, when he grabbed it, framed it
sang it, for us,
all of it to all of us.
We gladly surrendered.

***

In the end, no life remained at Crawford Grill—
only a barricade through which to peer.
After the fire, old patrons saw back-hoes appear
heard their slow crash and grumble—
first windows, then doors to happier years
were razed to make way for the Arena shine
and Civic[10]mind, "pure" and round and white.

One Day in "Black September"— 1972 Munich Olympic Games[11]

One winter by and here again the same:
a flake of snow that started with the rain.
The world now white, the blood congealed by cold,
seventeen corpses down and three let go.

Not for Greece those frozen tears were shed,
for years ago Olympia turned dead.
But rather for that game You would not see,
though some still claim You're clear by prophecy.

Oh, bearded One, did You then pluck Your eyes?
They'll not be caught; the frozen dead not rise.
The winter's come, the spotless blanket spread,
and in Your white, the pure, impaled, lie dead.

So now Old Wizened Man, where will You go?
Your children's tears singe red beneath the snow!

Glass Ceilings: 9/11/01

They ran for all their might,
   these women of the world,
who had worked overtime to climb
   through their glass ceilings.

Accountants, executives, do-it-all women,
   families at home, children in day care,
husbands beside them—
   partners in progress,
stockbrokers, secretaries,
   they knew the ropes:

breakfast at five,
   dressed by six,
children up by seven,
   out of the house by eight,
at work by nine, sharp!

And then the unimaginable:
   fire   cacophony   chaos!

Their glass ceilings came crashing down.

In the maelstrom of smoke and limbs
   they scrambled down the stairs
then ran for their lives,

clutching their purses.

Emergency Room

Don't ask me what I feel
and forget to look in my eyes,
forget to hear my voice, or even
listen to my pleas for help—
Don't tell me you will be back
and then forget to come,
forget what I said,
if ever you heard—
Don't tell me you will relieve
my pain then walk,
disappear for an hour,
to leave that vomit-sour aching
taste in my mouth, that tremor
to shake in my hands and heart, all
the while awaiting that minute
when I thought you would come,
would assuage my hurt, my grief.
Will trust return? Can I trust
you— your intent, your words
when you've gone away, awry?
I will weigh your empty face
and take my pangs, my head
in hands, hold my breath,
and turn my mind to another time
when stars might come,
lift me up toward another realm.

Happy Hour

The venerable Grief requests your company
at his parlor, hour one to five;
you need not come, but please RSVP
so he will know to count you still alive.

Newly parted lovers, sunshine friends
will all be there to shake— the final truce—.
Of course, in order not to make amends
each will come prepared with his excuse

to decorate the end. So all will turn
and twist, and eyes yet blinded pin the tail.[12]
Then, prizes for the able who discern
felicities of gray, the face most pale.

Come one! Come all! Attend this happy hour;
No need with Grief to cry, or sulking, cower.

Somewhere on Some Absolute Rung

When I was young
I only climbed my ladder up,
up to the leaves
in my tree-house,
up to the wispy clouds
that held my floating dreams,
higher yet to the seams
between enchanting choices
that mom and dad called
my iridescent voice.

Time paused at no single rung,
restive seconds sang their songs.

Yet, in some absolute hour
the ladder turned.
Was it upside down? No, I would say not.
Did it flip or disobey? No, no—
Nor did the rungs quick break.
Not exactly—
But the steps only allowed
a downward way with slowing hours,
backward minutes, and a drift of body,
a bewildered soul.

Oh You Fingers

Oh you fingers, you—
how do you wear
out, how
do you twist with time
bend from age
and lack of bond
to youth?
Why no soothe
of pain, no calm of heat
nor heal of joint
but only screams
of red, purloined from bleak
of days, from cold
of nights and stretched
by vein and voice
of sorrow?

I Forgot

You have to begin to lose your memory if only
in bits and pieces, to realize that memory is
what makes our lives. Life without memory is
no life at all... our memory is our coherence.
— from "My Last Sigh" by Luis Bunuel

I forgot
your name today
forgot your voice until we talked,
the kind timbre, resonance of your words,
your thoughtfulness—these I didn't forget.

I forgot the time of the group,
our poetry group, the names of the members
their faces, where they're from,
even the kind of poems they write,
but when they started to read
I knew each one, his gentle touch,
her loving words, their strong memories,
prescient memories.

I could recall some
sunsets last month
on the lake in Michigan—
the magenta clouds, the pinking skies
their pinching orange sun
when he wept toward the west,
and all the while, eyed
his uprising moon,
the auburn shadowed one—

All these memories
then blended together, coalesced
into a single silver orb,
before they slivered
to shards once more,
as my dimming days forgot again—
lost their mirror
to a shattered glass
of fractured, mangled time.

Lost in the Gibbous Night of Evening—

After our sail, after the end of our affair
       I took the lid off my mind,
juggled his slights, our fling, my fright—

His duty it was to shake his memories clear
       cover his anonymous grin
and lose it in the crumbling rock and ruins.

Such a small town, such a holiness of grief,
       emerging from our rain-soaked beach
traversed only by his wretched wisp of wench.

Lost in the gibbous moon of night,
       I searched far among the wimpled nuns.
Among the medieval priests I looked.

But in no way could I find a clarity
       of thought, nor right my keel
and come about into dawn's waxing light.

Your Next Journey

When first you breathless told of your haunting trip
the ravens hovered, clouded, gleaming black.
With quickened thoughts, I winced emerald hot,
shuddered, just thinking of your thundering plight.

When again, breathless, you told of your haunting trip,
the lake and sky both glowered cold and grim.
Clarity forgot its thought, no light to limn,
and sunrise submerged to moonless, dour night—

So now I'll inquire with you right next to me,
Why do you, here mired in memory,
ask me to join and be a central part?
"Live it up," you say, but I just cannot

see how this will wrap my heart in velvet
suede, assuage all anguish, set me free.

Collage

After the hurricane, the deluge
of drops and days, we wondered
if it might happen again,
if the cerise and ocher blue
would collage the sky taupe/black,
could crack and turn
the heavens and clouds
askew, and on their side.
We pondered at the cause—
what was true,
what right,
and if either might
ever refract and bend
to a single speck,
or single beacon of light.

Tears—
Harvey, Irma and Chiapas—9/8/2017;
Maria, 9/20/2017

Tonight, heavy now the leaves
judder their drops
heavy into morning they tear
they tear the fronds off
their palms, their plaintive boughs
until nothing is left—
nothing but silence shears the air
the quivering of a lone mare
her shaking
the shuddering and silence

Between My Words

I think now about those spaces between
my words, those spaces that hide my thoughts,
my fears, my dreads that I don't share.
How can I really, when they might reveal
an alarm at life, at death, of which even
I am unaware. I think of that space,
the dark matter, the missing light
where black holes reside— tempt
and torment my trembling, toss
my hiding place of stutter and blank
between no words— I pause at no thought,
at empty, at hungry

Defining Syllables

How to know a syl-
   lable—where to start,
what sounds, how round,
   where does it break?
Does it quake? The broken re-
   sound of moments
in time: yours, mine,
   anyone's, when pieces
don't connect
   just snipe—
snippets, splits
   of fractals and ice—
frozen in form,
   foreign diction,
airy slices of life.

The Raccoon Ball

I watched it all day out the window
at kindergarten—
I'm sure of it, Mom.
It was sunny, no rain, no clouds.
I could see it for sure,
the gym next door,
all those inside rooms.
And there it was, the black
and round raccoon ball, pounding
one wall, then the next.
And they all kept crashing down
when that big old ball kept hitting
the doors, the windows, and building sides
after it swinged way up.
Boy mom, I could really see it.
Even furniture, Mom, smashed into pieces!
I saw a yellow truck
on the ground and a little man
working levers—two or three—.
And, oh yeah, I saw
a couple of long lines
close up to the sky, before
they 'tached on that one last lever—
Really high, it was, I swear it,
before those long lines came down
and 'tached again to the raccoon ball,
all big all black, which swinged
wider, stronger, wilder.
The rooms went to small pieces.

Doors cracked, too
tiny splinters of wood.
All more and more a wreck.

Mugsi and Her Shadows

With scarce a glance back at her
former self, our substandard,
standard poodle, Mugsi, looks

like she is a show dog— just small
and curly-black against the emerald
grass. With body poised, left

front leg raised, she waits, waits,
(pitched still and steady) for the next
bird's shadow. It started with a dragon

fly, her brown eyes trained
across the shore, not near,
not far, just here at the lake,

in the wait, the watch
for the next swift, brown-
gray shape darting, first slow,

then fast, just beyond her grasp.
She'd watch the chickadees,
the butterflies, the orioles,

then spring across the marigolds,
through the forest, and leap again
to catch their winged shadows—

since hers are the essential
shades of time, the fleeting
spirits and evanescent sprites of life.

With Grace, The Seasons

With Grace, The Seasons

For Charlie

With grace the flakes fell and covered the empty
fields of autumn, offering us time beside the fire

to read, and see, each the graying other anew,
with searching eyes more wide, opening full

to desire, to thirst— to yearn. Never would
we retreat, nor for that matter could, though

rather met the fire full on, engaged as we were
for days, until you (or was it I?) noticed buds

upon the trees and from our cocoon,
as winged monarchs, flew out to greet

the spring. Rain and wind blustered clouds across
our sky, opened narcissi to gold, as redpolls returned

to find their home. Our feet ambled new paths
whilst your arm draped slant across my back—

Oft-times, my hand, true even my mind, slipped
inside of yours. We almost forgot to feel our summer,

except the heat again, which we already knew. Then,
once again through the solstice light, the air warm still

with its embrace of long days of summer, my eyes
sought yours and waited— as we hoped for the return

of our flickering days of youth, those days we lay
on flaxen beds of hay— prickling, yet tender—

and wished to be rolled forever into one
single bale to last the winters through.

Chiaroscuros

Dancing their world like dappled ghosts
my shadows dissipated to chiaroscuros —

fleeting images
of moon yielded slowly
to dawns of warmer days

as frozen fields broke
                from their fright
                        and shimmied forward
                                to sun.

Then sunflowers, wheat
                budded
                        up to glimmering dreams —

Unfolding seams of life
                and mind
                        bloomed to flower

at first with hesitance,
                at first in shade, and then into a frisson

of Light as she opened her wings
                                to spring.

Only then could I hear
                shining ripples of Time,
                                the horizon
                                        on her salty breath,

her silver terns swooping

as seconds ticked
        into a glow
              of glittering song.

Fibonacci's Secret

Of Nefertiti, the queen of the golden

mean, two rabbits asked
What color a number?

But one month later
there were three rabbits to ask.
Then as she turned her back for one

month more, to worship the golden
sun there were already five,
then, sure enough, eight to inquire
as they hopped behind
Egyptian-blue delphinium stalks.

Out the other side
they numbered thirteen
as they nestled
at the root of mustard
corn marigolds
with their thirteen petals,
tipped by linen cream white.

One month to the day
the hares darted to chicories, azure
chicories, whose petal numbers
matched the coffee brown
creature's: twenty-one in all.

Nefertiti never knew
of conch shells,
the elegance of their spiral,
of DaVinci, Mozart, Bartok,
nor, for that matter, had she
given much thought
to copulating rabbits.
She had never heard
of the stock market.[13]

Vespers of Fireflies

Just at the height of the twilight
                    as the waning eve was ceding
her wandering purple rays
                    and the clamor of cicadas whistled
their clicks together
                    in raucous unison,
                                        quick flickers
of beams shifted on
                    then off,
                                then appeared
                                        once again,
                                                    as if
a four year old
            had just been given
                        a brand new
                                    flashlight
                                        (a tiny one for sure)
and all the while delighted
                    in jumping
                            from creaking log
                                        up to rock
                                                    then down
                    to swampy bog,
each second switching
                    his winking wand
                            on,
                                    then off,
                                        then on
                                                    once more

in a brand new spot—
        even as the gray veil
              of dark
carefully placed
      her dew-soaked dome
           around the hemlocks,
their enticing, zesty scent,
        and the preying,
           croaking
              frogs.

A Picture

Maybe it comes down to this: a nugget
of kindness fished from misery's stream...
—from "Endurance" by Michelle Bitting

I will wake,
the pain will scratch
and scramble my back,
ache my hips,
wake me from the tempting
truths of dreams, their
dancing dalliances, dizzying
waves of deep, and catch
my eyes first, to gaze
at this, a picture, oak trees dancing,
burnished leaves dropping,
and new slips of sunlight making
their way through the mist,
the hay-mist around a barn—
and then again the hips,
damned if they don't hurt—
before I step outside
with my cane,
to greet the *Rose hips*,
the last of the summer's *Daylilies*,
and the *Rudbeckia*, their name
always ruder than their twinkling
center, ebony black— mocked
by their gold, harvest-glow gold
petals and a lake so blue

you might mistake it
for a late summer sky.

Tiffany's Reflections

How many panes I couldn't discern
when I turned to look
then looked again during this
gloaming solstice night— and where
did he conceive how the baby
blues, the mauves and magenta
pinks would reflect, refract
and take their place next
to gamboge golds, watermelon
greens? Such tiny slivers, empty
fragments by themselves, yet each facet
elegant beside the other, spaced
in design to receive its own
beam, its own glint
in the race against a dying day.
Who would know that light
could so affect a face?

Even the crickets

crochet my sight—

I cannot write
about what I see
from the porch after orioles
parachute from pines to cedar
and embellish water-clear
sky with sibilant tulip-bloom
voice and tune, while long-
shed shadows sing
far below.

Rather, I should not write
how maples pigment green
grass dandelions as they grasp
up to reach each birdsong's feather.

Yes, late still while the sun
ablaze takes her toll—

my sight now blurry
perhaps more than weary—

I must convert these eyes
to ears, focus on the crickets—
their buzz, the humming-
birds, the thrum of red-winged
black ones even
the whistle of unnamed flying

stripes and the whippity trill
of Connecticut's warblers.

No, I shall not write
but only listen —

hew to these unknown
poems, these aerial words.

North American Birds— A Saunter Through an Index on *Shore Birds*—

1. Sanderling

So who named you
and why, Ms. Sanderling?
Were you a'sauntering
in the sand, or a'skipping
to see your friend, Ms. Ling,
hoping for a little bread
on her grassy-land, when here
she gets this idea to place
her order for a name
with Mr. Audubon, who tells
her to kill you out-right
just like he does all those
beautiful birds he describes, kills,
then draws at dusk or dawn —

Yes, who was it? Ms. Ling, or
the murderer, Mr. Audubon?

2. American Bittern

How did you evolve
to find your food
(at once so savory good?)
to bob along the sandy shore
and find enough and evenmore from marram harsh
and prickly grass surround?

Through the glass I see
only your long bill and wonder
if true to your name,
by the time the periwinkles
reach your gullet, they taste bitter
but if by magic you
convert them to a taste
so rich and sweet that even
honey can't compete.

3. Plover

I think that all over
you are white, at least in winter
snow but no matter, to me
you wander the spaces
I most like to be,
the great lakes' beaches,
their far reaches, with
windswept expanses, desolate
and free and only land-
waves, years of water,
even wild grass to contain
your comrades along the endless
shore, and a few cormorants
in the lacy, lazy sky.

4. Kildeer

Why would they call you,
a tiny shore bird, a killing
deer, you who could barely

kill anything, except perhaps
a snail or two, or tiny
mollusks. I think
of you and your slim
black beak and wonder who
names birds and what
their motives in life,
and if, in your case, they—
like Mr. Audubon—
always have murder
on their mind.

5. Ruddy Turnstone

No matter I haven't
seen a photo of you,
I get the picture, you
must be red, or some
version of it— at least
ruddy complected— or so
thought some bird-watcher
some time ago,

but turnstone, hey,
that is the catch—
is that like turncoat,
but different? Did you
betray some birdwatcher
or more likely your feathered
friends in arms?

6. Sandpiper

Now finally I
can write a poem
about a bird
where the name
is understandable,
a bird that messes
around in sand,
has a good time doing it,
chases along the shore
(with its oh so skinny legs)
to skirt the waves—
and pipes its enormous
beak (for its tiny size)
into the sand to grab
a morsel of god knows what,
before skittering away
from the next breaking wave.

7. Willet

Will it run into the great
lakes, feet and skinny legs
first, to plunge its beak
into the sand or catch
insects drawn to the waves'
edge? Will it chase other birds
away from their nests
along the cruel, unforgiving
coastline. Will it find
Monica Willet and ask her

why she gave it her moniker?
We will never know. Not even
in the rain, nor falling snow.

8. Lesser Yellowlegs

What I want to know
is whether you have a cousin
who lives further north,
and carries the name of *greater
yellowlegs*. Or a brother
or sister, longer-legged perhaps,
who lives among the reeds
and graying rocks and is called
bigger gray-green-legs. Now
that would be a mouthful
to be sure, but so, too, are all
these mystical, nonsensical names

9. Dunlin

I could have gone
and done lent you
my name and then I
would have known
what you looked like
and why some crazy
guy decided to name you
after himself, instead,
but here he gave us no hint
of color nor nothing, nor
choice to lend our name.

He done lent his own,
and we are done
out of luck. We know you
live on the shore, but that
is all— except, when you
are done in, to wish you well.

10. American Woodcock

Well, now, at least here
we have somewhere
and something to go on.
We know what country
from which you hail,
and either, *either* you
are made of wood, or
just as likely you hang out
around shore and wood.
But who, *just who,* can easily
imagine a cock being around
the woods at the shore, unless
there is a forest close
to the shore, which,
come to think of it, is
a possibility, unless we
are talking about a totally
different type of cock!

Fall Again,

And the sun speaks only
to trees, echoes off
turning leaves when they catch
bright whirls of wind—
while starlings, caramel brown,
sneak between blowing seeds
and ruckus of gilded, locust coins—
as squirrels patter on branches,
chase to nearby tips, then quick
hurl to hawthorns as if
in trespass by the sky,
all to catch the season's spin
of pinwheel colors—
tangerine, burnished bronze,
            ocher red—
as they fall
            again.

The Equinox Has Quickly Passed

and trail by chevron trail, the bragging geese
are flying south, competing in course and speed
with the hummingbirds whose throats now match
the loud and crimson fronds of fiery sumacs

and brazen canopies of maples' flash —
those sugary carmine ones, who sneak to steal
the anthocyanin and chlorophyll
from these rusting scarlet plants — their hidden stash.

The equinox has passed, as tauping grass
and stalks of dying corn both scrap in their race
to burlap the fading fields, their surly faces
about to scream from a growing fall crevasse:

Beware, the nights, their frost to come, their snow,
Beware the cold, the ebony of crows!

Giving Thanks

Let's give thanks
that we are here
once more

to sing in praise

of puffins,
pin oaks,
apple muffins,
a dust of snow.

For a whole year
beyond and past:
tomorrows turned
to yesterdays
and yesterdays yet to come,

let's sing our praise.

Memory's Fragments

From beyond the bridge, beyond our thoughts
our rill kept her flow, the leaves dropping
no shadows from above, no whispers of amber fall
below— but only small fragments of other times
their moments and memories of song
voiced long ago into terse seconds—
their current of rivers, minutes of days,
as they ghosted their way
to an undertow of ocean rime.

Snow Cold

His days awoke
to an algid winter,
the solstice barely
piercing the pines,
as the fade
of day buried
her violet retreat,
slow first
and then fast,
never to catch the night
nor even touch
the scent, the crouch
of dawn.

Come with me,

get in and shut the door
you don't need any more
woe of city winter, her
ghosts of frost, coats of snow,
trellised on your window panes.

Come with me and shut the door
on tangled skeins of scattered days,
their brambled knots of pent-up ways.

Come take a ride;
we'll go north
to where the mountains start
to cross our trail—

North, where the greening blue of lakes
re-make our eyes, fasten our feet
to soil of scenes we'll never forget—
among skies which toss drifts
of clouds into our midst,
and mist our eyes
to tears,
to night, to joy.

Come,
shut the door.
We just might
have to get lost.

Lesbos

In memory of Alan Kurdi, September 2, 2015

Up onto the rocky shore they washed,
small bodies interspersed between
delphinium blue and brilliant
breaking waves, which tumbled
from the Aegean water, the sky —

but no one new knew their names

Up onto the rocky shore they washed,
yellow life-jackets that were only toys,
never promised to be devices
for flotation, for rescue,
never promised to save lives —

but no one knew whose lives, what names

Up on the rocky shore break more waves,
more small bodies without names,
families lost;
no play in the summer sun,
no splashing by the sea-shore.

No one knows their names.

At the Jetty

It was the haar of the sea
we heard— then the gulls,
their shiver, as they swooped
stealing the fog,
drawing it in and down
beyond the dusk, the damp,
the cage of cold—

and at the shore
the line of silver
birches, peeling—
pummeling the wind
and our now vacant souls.

These three years—

dark days, deceit of meaning
month after month—
weeks of winters twisting
their bare, foreboding arms.

No chocolates, no sweet
potatoes, nor magnolias,
daffodils come spring;
only the coldest winters of snow.

Words too many
for doctors to write
in tomes of tattered pages—
long since torn, scattered.

Days and months—
time and seconds taut,
while answers absent, elusive
float only in doubt.

Waiting rooms broadcast
show after show: Wolf,
the View, the Talk
camouflage all agony, all angst.

My doctor suggests a walker,
"exercise equipment," he opines—
while I hold my mask, place it
with care around my face.

More anguish
than a soul could know
more struggle
than a poem can own.

The Days That Have Left Me

These are my wildest hours
of surrender,[14] where my minutes tick
my clock back to midnight
and the seconds get too close
to black, to bleak.

These are the days that have left
me— blind, in a flurry of wasted
soul, a body yearning for rest
away from the searing pain
that scorches to flame.

I tell only of the wrench
and wrest of limb from limb,
the wish to be free
and alight on pine needles
under full cover of lilac
evening, rocked in a cradle
of molten moonlight.

Gravity

Caught amidst the asteroids,
stars, earth and sun,
our cratered, lunar orb
shed its long shadows

down the road,

from one of us,
five feet and more
down the hill
to the other—
even brightened our
stubble-frosted fields,

and, for an instant,

gave us
gentle reprieve
from winter's dark,
from the loss of day's glow,
until a coyote's howl

punctured the repose—

until the corpse
of our neighbor (shot
straight through the brain)
surfaced face down—
his ripped and bloody

red flannel jacket
covered in white frost.
Likely a midnight toss
of body into the caustic
cold of snowy copse.

Today, Of White[15]

Today my bones shudder and shake—
quake with the wanton cold of winter
her snows of white and wasted draft
her fugitive clouds laughing across
a prairie of blank— empty,
as we wait for a sparkle of spring
that just won't thaw.

Today is barely a week after
the solstice when the air is paper thin
difficult to breathe—
only ice crystals to see
and foggy froth from mouth
to air and back
if luck will have it so.

And yet into a new year I trudge
step by frozen step, my mind
inches forward as I image
that one emerald blade of grass
that amber sun push her way
to nudge a nascent pinking horizon
into her new moments of dawn.

Our Snow Cave

This is the true religion, the religion of snow,
and sunlight and winter geese barking in the sky,
I say, but he is too busy to hear me.
—from "Shoveling Snow with Buddha" by Billy Collins

I know that Billy Collins wrote
about shoveling snow with the serene Buddha
along a cold and misty driveway, and how they

shared (if you could call it that) a conversation
about their arduous work that bright
and sparkling day with "fountain bursts of snow."

But I wonder if Billy ever stood inside
our snow cave and witnessed the light
we saw right inside, and, too, what he imagined

was going on just there— with the snow
reflecting off the surface of the fields,
and the Buddha (where we kids had

only constructed a snow man, just
a plain one, no special name, nor nothing—),
and did Billy think there was a new

Buddha being born inside our cave
when the ice-light shone blue and burned
a hole right there inside his shoes?

As Embers Burn

Tonight I don't see her head
as Mugsi lies on the couch
black paws outstretched
twitching ears flopping her
pillow with dreams
perhaps of skunks she evaded
when I called
and she wouldn't come
all hot on a trail

Tonight I don't see her face
all wrapped in a beige
furry coat, 10 years beyond
all expectation of life, soft,
sweet and tender life—
Tuffy, who has lost
her last meow, but draws,
pulls us in by pointing with body,
with feet weakened
by splaying and aged ankles
life insistent

Tonight I don't see his voice
silenced by Django,
Django's stunning lift,
his play with Stéphane,
but I hear Charlie
listening
through the room
by the fireplace

thoughts penetrating—
encapsulating our lives,
our family, our night.

Echoes—

Echoes of Solstice Light Beginning

That was the night the sky breathed
light and in her breath the lake was born
her waves mingling the rime
whispers of dusk into lapping sleep—
silent licks of memory's voice

that was the night of a shining crescent
and clouds which blew fragrant stars
into redstarts of day
gave us glistening chimes of sun
bright upon a life of love

and we knew we had to remember
these echoes— no choice but to hold them.

Notes

1 Adapted from "Sometimes, I Am Startled Out of Myself," from *Radiance* by Barbara Crooker. Word Press, 2005.

2 Inspired by "You Too Got Tired" by Yehuda Amichai.

3 Serge Kovaleski is a disabled reporter whom Trump made fun of during his campaign for president.

4 A "murmuration" refers to the phenomenon that results when hundreds, even thousands of starlings fly in swooping, intricately coordinated patterns through the sky.

5 The butterfly effect is the concept that small causes can have large effects. Initially, it was used with weather prediction, but later the term became a metaphor used in and out of science. In chaos theory, the butterfly effect is the sensitive dependence on initial conditions in which a small change in one state of a deterministic nonlinear system can result in large differences in a later state. —adapted from Wikipedia

6 "Try to Keep your Heart Open" was inspired by a poem by Lynne Knight, "Try to Keep your Heart Open," in *Rattle's Poets Respond*, January 3, 2017.

7 Between 1939 and the end of April, 1945, over 130,000 female prisoners passed through the Ravensbrück concentration camp, a camp built just for women. By the time the Russians had liberated the camp at the end of April, 1945, between 20,000 to 30,000 of the women had perished in Ravensbrück, a town whose name is literally translated as "raven's bridge." This poem was written on April 30, 2015, seventy years after the liberation of Ravensbrück.

8 *Fuji*, in Japanese, means *unparalleled*, or *unequalled*, or *never-ending*.

9 Charles "Teenie" Harris (1908-1998) was born in Pittsburgh, Pennsylvania, the son of hotel owners in the city's Hill District. Early in

the 1930s he purchased his first camera and opened a photography studio. From 1936 to 1975, Harris chronicled life in the black neighborhoods of the city for *The Pittsburgh Courier,* one of America's oldest black newspapers. The body of his work constitutes one of the largest photographic documentations of a minority community in the United States. His work was rarely seen outside of Pittsburgh, until after his death in 1998. In addition to his photo essays of daily life in the city, he captured many celebrities who visited Pittsburgh, from musicians such as Louis Armstrong, Duke Ellington, Lena Horne and Sarah Vaughan to notable figures such as John F. Kennedy and Martin Luther King. Harris also photographed legendary Negro League baseball players.—adapted from Wikipedia

10   The Civic Arena in Pittsburgh was a white-domed hockey rink that also served as a performance hall and hosted numerous concerts, the circus, political and religious rallies, roller derbies, and contests in basketball, wrestling, lacrosse, football, ice skating championships, kennel shows, and soccer. It was built after the African American district known as the "Hill District" was razed for the purpose of building it. It was in existence from 1961 until 2011 when it, too, was demolished.

11   This poem was penned when I was stranded at home by an early winter blizzard in Boulder, Colorado— September 5-6, 1972, as the news of the Munich massacre was first making its way to the ears of those of us in the United States.

12   Pin the tail on the donkey is a common game played at children's birthday parties and sometimes adult gatherings as well. A picture of a donkey with a missing tail is tacked to a wall within easy reach of children. One at a time, each child is blindfolded and handed a paper "tail" with a push pin or thumbtack poked through it. The blindfolded child is then spun around until he or she is disoriented. The child gropes around and tries to pin the tail on the donkey. The child who pins the tail closest to where it belongs on the donkey is the winner.

13   The following is the Fibonacci series: 0, 1, 1, 2, 3, 5, 8, 13, 21, 34, 55, 89, 144…Each number is derived from adding the two previous numbers

in growing succession, starting at zero. The ratio of each successive pair of numbers in the series approximates phi (1.618. . .), as, for example, 5 divided by 3 is 1.666..., and 8 divided by 5 is 1.60. After the 40th number in the series, the ratio is accurate to 15 decimal places. The number which is derived is called phi; this is considered to be the "divine" or "golden" number. It is 1.618033988749895.

This number is found in many aspects of nature, and many artists have utilized it in drawing, sculpting and the like, as they have used the "golden mean," the ratio of 1 to this imaginary number. Nefertiti, an Egyptian Queen who lived in approximately 1400 B.C. was said to exhibit inordinate beauty because her face had many measurements that followed to perfection the "golden mean" and "golden ratio." From the "golden ratio" or "golden mean" is derived a "golden rectangle" through which a "golden spiral" is derived, evident in, for example, the conch shell or even spider webs. Leonardo de Vinci painted Mona Lisa's face to fit perfectly into a golden rectangle, and structured the rest of the painting around similar rectangles. Mozart divided a striking number of his sonatas into two parts whose lengths reflect the golden ratio, though there is much debate about whether he was conscious of this. In more modern times, Hungarian composer Bela Bartok similarly followed the golden ratio.

The number of petals in a flower is often one of the following Fibonacci series numbers: 1, 2, 3, 5, 8, 13, 21, 34 or 55, or sometimes even a combination of the above. If a rabbit pair begins each month to copulate, with one pair at the start of a month, and there are no deaths, the number of pairs of rabbits in the field at the start of each month is 1, 1, 2, 3, 5, 8, 13, 21, etc. It is interesting to note that the Fibonacci series has been used as a tool to analyze the stock market and as a helpful, albeit complex, strategy to utilize when planning how and when to invest. And finally, though there are many other examples of Fibonacci's number exhibited in nature, they are not included in this poem.—adapted from Wikipedia

14 With a nod to Joseph Hermitage for "wildest hour of surrender."

15 After "Early Spring Thaw" by Di Brandt.

Acknowledgements

Acknowledgements

I would like to express my gratitude to Julie Albright who has worked graciously and tirelessly with me as an editor in helping me bring this book to fruition.

Secondly, I would like to thank my son, Ariel Brice, and Jim Hutt for their work on the book cover and front cover photograph by "Villager Jim" of Derbyshire, UK whose alluring "Clarissa" image captures a starling murmuration above the village of Great Longstone in Derbyshire, England.

Finally, I would also like to thank the following print and online journals who have chosen to help my poetry see the light of day and come to the eyes of readers. For them and their decisions to publish my work, I am most grateful:

Annals of Internal Medicine (July 3, 2018): Emergency Room.

Bear River Review: Our Snow Cave (2013), To Charlie Beyond the Mist (2013) Even the Crickets (2016), Berries Bittersweet (2017)

Paterson Literary Review: Somewhere on Some Absolute Rung, Death's Bridge, I Forgot (2017), The Circle Closes (to be published Spring 2019) chosen as Editor's Choice in the Allen Ginsberg Poetry Contest, 2018

Vox Populi: No Moon Shadows; Collage; Call Me Simple— a poem in honor of Serge Kovaleski; (reprinted in *Nasty Women & Bad Hombres: A Poetry Anthology*—November and Padolf, Lascaux Editions) (2017); Today, Of White (2018)

Versewrights.com: Overhead from Longing (2017) Chiaroscuros (2017); The Raccoon Ball (2016); Lesbos (2016) At the Jetty (2016); Mourning Calls (2016); These Three Years (2017)

Tuckmagazine.com: His *Butterfly Effect*, Tears— Harvey, Irma and Chiapas —9/8/2017; Maria, 9/20/2017, Glass Ceilings (2017)

Finally, I would like to thank Tony Manfredonia, a Petoskey, Michigan composer, who elected to set the words of *Mourning Calls* to music for quintet and baritone. The masterful world debut was performed in Pittsburgh, PA on December 12, 2017 by the Tuesday Musical Club and can be heard at https://soundcloud.com/tony-manfredonia/sets/mourning-calls .

About the Author

Judith Alexander Brice is a retired Pittsburgh, PA psychiatrist whose love of nature, experiences with illness, both her own (including Crohn's disease, multiple surgeries and severe, debilitating pain) and that of her patients, has informed much of her work. She has been writing poems for many years, but started writing more assiduously and taking workshops and writing classes about 15 years ago.

Her over 45 published poems have appeared previously in *The Lyric, The Paterson Literary Review, The Pittsburgh Post-Gazette, The Bear River Review, Vox Populi.com* and *Versewrights.com*, among many other national publications. One poem, "Questions of Betrayal," appears as well in a book about the Palestinian-Israeli conflict titled *Before There Is Nowhere to Stand.* And one of her poems has been made part of the permanent collection of the Holocaust Memorial Center in Farmington Hills, MI.

Her first book of collected poems, *Renditions in a Palette,* was published in 2013 by David Robert Books. One poem from this current collection, "Mourning Calls," has been published in *Versewrights.com* and also has been set to music by Tony Manfredonia. The inaugural performance of this quintet with voice was in Pittsburgh on December 12, 2017. It was performed by The Tuesday Musical Club and can be heard online at https://soundcloud.com/tony-manfredonia/sets/mourning-calls .

Judy Brice divides her time between Pittsburgh and Petoskey, MI where she lives with her husband, Charlie, also a poet, and their poodle (no, not groomed to look like a freak!) and her two cats.

Made in the USA
Lexington, KY
20 August 2018